Dec 2013

Dear Marian —

One of my favorite
cat-lovers.

Happy Birthday!

Love,
Cindy

From the outset, I have sought to celebrate primarily stray, adopted, shelter, and foster Cat Angels. There are a few "pure" breeds in this collection, but even some of these were from rescue organizations. I feel it is vitally important to honor the lost, forgotten, and forsaken, the animals who truly need our help: no angel should ever be abandoned.

Cat Angels

The Secret Lives of Cats

Amy White

CAT ANGEL
PRESS

CAT ANGEL PRESS
P.O. Box 2267
FAIRVIEW, NC 28730
www.catangels.com

Published by
CAT ANGEL PRESS
P.O. Box 2267, Fairview, NC 28730
www.catangels.com

a division of
FAIREWOOD STUDIOS, LLC
www.fairewood.com

ISBN 978-0-9825864-9-5

Design by Dan Schuman, Lawrence Marie, Inc.
Printed in the USA with soy-based inks on forest stewardship council-certified paper
by BookMasters, Inc., Ashland, Ohio, January 2010, job print number M6821
Direct-to-Consumer Distribution by AtlasBooks

All photomontages © 2010 Amy White

The vast majority of all photographic elements are © 2010 Amy White.
Many of Amy's photographs are represented by and available for purchase through
The National Geographic Stock Image Collection, and SPI.
www.nationalgeographicstock.com

A few photographic elements incorporated into some of these
photomontages were drawn from Corel Stock imagery. Therefore, some of these
photomontages have co-copyright credit to acknowledge the author's use of
these few photographic elements from Corel stock.

So, in addition to © 2010 Amy White, there is also

© 2010 Corel (for the following photomontage elements as listed below):
The background image in: The Magic Lantern, Jackie on Halloween,
Buddha Cat, Wizard Cat, Rites of Spring, Mt. Rushmeow, and Honoring our Ancestors.
The cat in: Buddha Cat, Moon & Star (Birman, left) Secrets (Turkish Van, left),
Kittens up a Tree (kittens), Head over Heels (Persian, right),
Got Fur? (Sphynx, left), and Cattaj Mahal.
And some wings: All owl and eagle wings and some of the song-bird wings.

Library of Congress Cataloging-in-Publication Data is available.

Disclaimer: some cats' names have been changed to protect the innocent.

Dedicated to my perfect partner in life, love, music & art
-my closest friend, my husband,
Al Petteway

and with thanks to all the Cat Angels that have gone before us:
St. Clair
Phooka
Zenobia
Noki
Tapioca
Rice Pudding
Tommy
Shi-Shi
Pomegranate
& Boots

Table of Contents

Introduction

———∙✦∙———

Whether dancing in celebration
of the coming season
or falling from grace,
or in your face,
Cat Angels are all around us,
inviting us to paws
and revel in the moment.

Come join this parade of
furry-feathered whimsy.
Discover the secret lives
of your own Cat Angels, and
listen to the stories they wish to tell.

Cat Angels

Everyone who has ever loved a cat has likely experienced the same suspicion: that cats are supernatural beings. Upright or fallen, obnoxious or sweet, it doesn't really matter—we can still sense their righteous, riotous natures and their devout other-worldliness.

In the most basic, chronological sense, cats are our unwitting angels because their life spans are inevitably shorter than our own. We witness their entire lives, knowing all the while that our time together is too brief.

THE MYSTICAL REALM & THE MEANING OF WINGS

The wings of Cat Angels represent their transient and transcendental nature. It's as if these wings are part gossamer soul and part tenth life - a subtly physical manifestation of angel powers. Cat Angels' wings are a passport for naturalized dual citizenship.

Cat Angels clearly belong in two places at one time: they belong here on this earth with us; and they also belong in that great mystical realm that they like to visit throughout their earthly lives, sometimes several times a day. Cat Angels only enter this mystical realm for good once they've left their ninth earthly life, and us, behind.

Depending on the Cat Angel, the mystical realm has any number of settings. It is often an amalgam of a typical heavenly place (complete with clouds and harps) and a healthy dose of reality—a holographic synthesis of all things mundane, fantastic and delicious, chock-full of things that are irresistible to a cat. The mystical realm can also provide a safe venue for confronting and exorcizing one's fears. It is often an accurate reflection of both a Cat Angel's inner spirit and outward appearance: everything from gorgeous, sensual, and whimsical, to dangerous or totally outrageous.

Once a Cat Angel reveals herself to you, consider yourself invited to embark on a wonderful journey and a remarkable learning experience. If you are willing to follow, your Cat Angel just may lead you into a beautiful new world. (Then again, if you haven't been giving her much attention lately, you might want to watch your step.) It's easy to be charmed and receptive to your cat's inner angel. If you try to see her, most of the time your Cat Angel will try to meet you half way.

ETHEREAL ADOPTIONS & GUARDIAN ANGELS

We are fortunate when our Cat Angels choose to spend their days with us. Once our hearts have been adopted, our Cat Angels can become our guardian angels and our spiritual guides. And we become their lucky charges.

Cat Angels continually watch over us. While playing "kitty parade" in front of the computer monitor; while sitting on the exact paragraph we are trying to read; even while looking on from a discrete distance with their eyes seemingly closed. Sometimes our Cat Angels may pretend to ignore us, or laugh at us to keep us humble. The greatest gifts from these Angels are their frequent teaching moments, their reminders about the more important things in life.

Cat Angels can be our catalysts. They encourage us to stretch our boundaries and our legs after a long nap.

Cat Angels encourage us to take risks and reach well beyond our earthbound ambitions for a world of fantastic possibilities, not to mention outright self-indulgence and silliness.

Cat Angels are our serendipitous spiritual guides. They remind us to search for peace within while urging us to play out with uninhibited passion.

By being our simultaneous beacons of light and paragons of silliness, our Cat Angels are always there to ensure we don't get lost in the dark. They don't want us to lose our way, or our senses of humor. When we dare to veer off course, our Cat Angels will be there to guide us back into gratitude, humility, and the proper practice of hedonism. They never want us to forget our many blessings.

While our Cat Angels know they've got it good, they take great pride in reminding us of our own good fortune. Naturally, they consider themselves to be chief among our many blessings. And we shouldn't have it any other way. 🐾

The First
Cat Angel

St. Clair was born near the stairs of the St. Clair guest house on the campus of Warren Wilson College, where my husband Al and I stayed for a week each summer. St. Clair was a bit scrawny when we first met, but she had picked a great place to be a stray, smack in the middle of the Swannanoa Gathering, a summer's worth of folk music camps whose friendly attendants were always generous with treats and food scraps.

Every morning, St. Clair would wait to greet me on the front porch, squinting hello in the early light, and we'd close out each day together with her lounging on my lap after she had polished off her latest meal. We spent more and more time together as the week progressed. Al and I soon considered her the mascot of the house, although we were pretty sure she had never been inside a house.

And St. Clair confirmed that the first time we tried to take her indoors. Whoa! Things were pretty rough that first half-hour, but once she detached herself from the ceiling and discovered the soft couch and the always-full food bowl, she decided all was well, and she didn't much care to go outside ever again. It seemed only fitting that St. Clair took on the name of her favorite haunt, since that was where her life began; that was where she had wooed us. And that was where our beautiful journey together commenced.

Unfortunately, St. Clair was in poor health: soon after she adopted us we learned she had feline leukemia. We gave her the best life we could for as long as we could, and she returned the favor in the way that only a rescued animal can, with a primal gratitude and an irresistible devotion.

I began documenting our relationship from the day we met and soon found that I couldn't stop. I photographed St. Clair almost daily to track her progress in hopes that this could somehow fortify her.

One day, St. Clair had commandeered my office chair and was upside-down, asleep. She was smiling and resplendent in a wonderful kind of twist. I photographed this moment of bliss—but when I took a second look at that setting, I realized the background left much to be desired. It seemed rather incongruous. There was my beautiful tabby subject: her expression was positively divine, and she was clearly in heaven. (Nearer to heaven, in fact, than I wanted her to be.) But something seemed different, and vaguely supernatural. Then it struck me: here was an angel!

I looked at St. Clair once more to confirm my impression. This time, I could see her flying in all her winged splendor. The effect was subtle, as if seen through a veil. It wasn't unlike that gentle thrill one encounters in the wood at twilight, when there are magic and mystery in the gloaming. Yet that image of St. Clair as angel seemed absolute to me. How could I not have noticed before?

This moment, this new way of seeing, this photograph, this cat's name and her very tenuous hold on existence - all of these conspired to reveal what St. Clair truly was: a Cat Angel. So I did what she seemed to ask of me: I enhanced her photograph to reveal her inner truth. I gave her wings and helped her transcend that office chair to take her rightful place in the sky. She rather liked the final result. And she seemed to insist that I do it again. And again. And again.

That's how my first Cat Angel took me by surprise. Then she took me by storm. No sooner had I discovered the angel in St. Clair, than I began noticing that same distinct angel-aura around all the other cats that crossed my path. These Cat Angels began to appear everywhere, asking to be discovered and celebrated. And they kept telling me about this mysterious hidden world that they loved to visit. They seemed anxious to tell me stories about their adventures and spiritual experiences on this "other side."

The spirit-stories of these many Cat Angels are the inspiration behind this collection.

I see the world differently now, thanks to the Cat Angels. Every setting is a potential palace. Every item is a potential toy or touchstone. And every interaction is a potential life lesson. Cat Angel elements are everywhere. I've made it my mission to photograph as many of these elements as possible and to distill them into their finest, whimsical essence, as the Cat Angels have requested of me. 🐾

———⟫●⟪———

With each image that follows, I am honoring the existence of our Cat Angels, as well as the bittersweet nature of the ephemeral in our lives.

ST. CLAIR

Angels can fly because
they take themselves lightly.

- G.K. Chesterton

The Great Adventure

―――⇒⊱⊰⇐―――

Have you ever noticed how some cats have a habit of staring at nothing in particular for hours at a time? Sometimes cats will even sit in front of something as plain as an interior wall, seemingly transfixed, their noses a mere inch from the paint. What do they find so interesting? Could it be a rodent on the other side of the drywall? The sound of a short in the electrical system?

And why is it that some cats insist on opening cabinet doors even when they know that these doors will not lead to their food or to the great outdoors? Don't cats know that a paper bag is just that? A paper bag?

The truth is that whenever cats are this intent on something, they are actually sensing the great opportunities on the other side of that wall and that cabinet door. They are seeing well beyond the portal of a crumpled paper bag.

This is where the angel dimension comes into play. Cat Angels have a unique sixth (or should that be tenth?) sense. Their angel vision enables them to survey vast landscapes beyond the common boundaries of our limited human, everyday world.

So, whenever we aren't looking, that's right where our Cat Angels will be: out and about, exploring their many alternate realities in pursuit of stories to share with their friends upon their return. 🐾

Paper Bag Portal

Confident, a bit smug, and more than a little winded, Stella rests with evidence of her latest foray into the mystical realm firmly in her grasp. The little rodent at the portal may think he's safe, but that impression, just like Stella's presence in the here and now, is only temporary.

Now you know where all of those leaves and the mystery debris come from: they are souvenirs from the other side! And perhaps that other realm is where all your missing socks have gone—not that you'll ever get them back. It's likely that most of our missing belongings have become keepsakes from the everyday world, stashed by our beloved Cat Angels for future sessions of extra-terrestrial play.

It is the eye which
makes the horizon.
- Ralph Waldo Emerson

Olson & the Moon

Even as a young angel, Olson knew his limits: none. The moon was as easy for him to reach as the giant crinkle-ball on the corner of the living room carpet. In fact, Olson is still convinced that the crinkle-ball and the moon are one and the same. Pieces of food long ago knocked from bowls and scattered about the house—those are the stars in his universe. And all those dust-bunnies? They are his wee furry nebulas, just begging to be explored. (The dust-bunnies that smell most distinctly of his own fur seem to be the most worthy of capture.)

Olson is so often lost in his own space that it is hard to know when he is truly here with us. Thankfully, Olson's sister Ryan has proven to be the best medium. Whenever Olson's head is too much in the mystical realm, Ryan will pounce on his unsuspecting body and he'll be right back with us again. Then those two inevitably tumble about on the carpet together, with stardust in their eyes.

Hope is the thing with
feathers that perches in the soul,
and sings the tune without words,
and never stops at all.
- Emily Dickinson

Hellion Angel

At times, Ellis can be quite the little hellion. He insists that loud pipes save lives, and loves to kick up the clouds in the mystical realm with his motor-bike. Other Cat Angels protest the noise, but Ellis insists that his pipes are just as valid an instrument as a trumpet or a harp, and his attitude and fishtail frolics are just as eloquent as the finest lyric—a valid contribution to the grand opus of life's conceptual, ambient orchestra.

So far, mostly due to his bad attitude, Ellis's campaign to make other Cat Angels accept the sound of his mystical bike hasn't gone all that well. Still, Ellis's non-biking buddies can't help but give him respect. Even though they are masters of their mystical realm, most Cat Angels harbor an innate fear of dogs as they travel between worlds, a trait inherited from instinct and from harried lives on earth.

Fortunately, Ellis has never suffered from this fear, and loves to give his dog-friends loud bike rides through the clouds, inspiring looks of envy and awe in his fellow Cat Angels as he goes riding by.

If we all did the
things we are capable
of doing, we would literally
astound ourselves.
- Thomas Edison

The Brass Ring

Houdini has a penchant for the dramatic. Whereas most Cat Angels slip in and out of their mystical realm almost imperceptibly, Houdini always insists on more presentation and flair. Nothing humdrum will do!

Houdini excels at taking everyday objects and turning them into elaborate touchstone portals. And he always insists on having an audience before entering his portals. Otherwise, why bother?

Houdini thinks Cat Angels take their trans-reality talents far too much for granted. His passion is to make every passage an event. He distributes gaudy, colorful fliers beforehand. And if there are not enough cats in attendance, Houdini cancels his passage.

At least that's his excuse. Most of Houdini's buddies actually think it's the other way around. They say that if too many Cat Angels show up for the passage, Houdini chickens out because the pressure is too great and he actually trips at the portal—a metaphysical hiccup, if you will.

Houdini's colleagues are more sympathetic than dismissive, though. They are a supportive bunch and don't mind too much that Houdini seems to be using excess hype to make up for his lack of finesse. They all love Houdini just the same. He's loads of fun in the mystical realm and is always worth the wait.

It is as easy to hold
quicksilver between
your fingers and thumb as to keep
a cat who means to escape.
- Andrew Lang

Jackie on Halloween

You'd never guess from this picture, but Jackie is quite the sweet and tame indoor-girl. Her people are loving parents of several full-time Cat Angels and dutiful foster parents of several more. Jackie leads a wonderful life on earth. She always feels secure as she moves from one sunbeam to another, content to cuddle and cavort with her Cat Angel siblings and view the curiosities of the world from behind the safety of a window.

But unbeknownst to her parents, Jackie's life in the mystical realm is in stark contrast to her earthly existence. Jackie's alternate persona is one of grand adventure and intrigue! She has a secret locker on the other side with enough dramatic capes, costumes, and gadgets to make a superhero jealous. And she uses them all.

Jackie's favorite haunt in the mystical realm is the rocky beach below the castle at Dark Cliffs. She perfects her sonar while flying with her bat cousins, skimming the surface of the waters and coming to rest, sometimes upside down, along the caves, cliffs and coves of the coastline.

While in the everyday world, there is little about Jackie to suggest her wilder, mysterious side. But every once in a while you can catch a glimpse of it. Jackie's gaze is often spirited with flames from her adventures in the mystical realm. It's all in the eyes.

We must walk
consciously only part way
toward our goal, and then leap in
the dark to our success.

- Henry David Thoreau

When in Rome

———⊷◈⊶———

In the mystical realm, all things are possible. That's what Tuxster found out on his first venture there. Ever since he was a wee kitten, Tux was smitten with the fish tank in his earthly home, a huge, colorful aquarium, full of brilliant, playful fish and hundreds of hypnotic bubbles. Tuxster would sit and daydream in front of this tank for hours. He loved to dream that he was living within its walls and that he was one with the fish, speaking in bubbles and dancing within that fluid school.

Whenever he tried to jump into the tank, Tuxster's humans thought he was trying to fish for dinner. They never caught on to his truly peaceful agenda. One day, on one of his more persistent balancing acts on the edge of the aquarium, Tuxster accidentally fell in and slipped right into the mystical realm. Instead of finding himself in the clouds (the most common landscape Cat Angels experience on their maiden voyage into the mystical realm), Tuxster found himself swimming among his beloved fishies.

Immediately, he felt as if he was part of the school, turning instinctively just as his fellow students did, skimming the surface for munchies, diving behind the vaguely authentic ruins at the least hint of startle. The fish were not frightened of him, and he wasn't the least bit interested in eating a single one of them, either. It was a beautiful thing!

Whenever he's in his mystical waters, Tuxster is beside himself with joy. He can never decide what's more appealing: being a part of this beautiful aquatic dance, wearing his fish mask, or actually being able to breathe in water.

If you
can't pretend,
you can't be king.

- Luigi Pirandello

The Magic Lantern

Like most Cat Angels, St. Clair loved to explore the mystical realm. That's where she gave her wings their best workout. And that's where she found her main passion in life: to find healing light and spread it throughout the universe.

St. Clair would venture to the farthest corners of her mystical realm to discover magical sources of light. Sometimes the light would be an aurora; sometimes it would be the flames of a campfire around which the finest music was played. Whenever she found this light, she would gaze upon its source to absorb its power and capture its essence in her enchanted lantern.

Upon returning to earth, St. Clair would find the moments and the people most in need of this light, and would shine before them until the darkness was gone. I know because she did this for me. There are times when I'm certain I can still see the glimmers of St. Clair's magical light, shimmering and sparkling around me.

Give light, and
the darkness will
disappear of itself.
- Desiderius Erasmus

Magic & Spirituality

Cat Angels recognize the inevitable cycle of life and death. They are a bit more matter-of-fact about this cycle than we are. Perhaps this is because from the moment they are born, Cat Angels have one paw placed firmly in that other world.

Some Cat Angels keep weaving in and out of that veiled portal. And who can blame them? They just want to see what's on the other side. In fact, Cat Angels don't usually bother differentiating between that ethereal door and the regular old door to your house that they keep having you open and close and open and close again. In the end, these two Cat Angel worlds are all the same to them.

Despite their very practical view of the here and now and the hereafter, Cat Angels are very reverent beings. They are deeply spiritual in nearly every respect. For example, Cat Angels always say grace, and they say it very well—but not just *before* a meal: they spread their gratefulness throughout the entire event. That serpentine dance around your legs as you prepare their food? That's part of the preamble. (There's some wing-fluttering, too, but it's much harder to perceive.)

There's also the stalking and harassing of the meal despite its already being dead. Then comes the purring, the licking of paws and face, and those squinty-eyed smiles and contented glances. Those are the closing phrases of grace after the meal has been consumed. And the inevitable post-meal nap? That is the Cat Angel Amen. (Cat Angels hold the record for the longest Amens in history.)

Don't be fooled into thinking that Cat Angels are traditionally religious. They are deeply spiritual, but in their own special, furry-feathered way. Ultimately, Cat Angels will answer to no one spirit, not even in the form of another Cat Angel. Of course they'll lie down and show their belly from time to time; it's only polite to acquiesce. But they'll pounce on that same spirit once it turns away again and isn't paying any attention. God, Spirit, and Feline are all the same to a Cat Angel. Everything is sacred. And everything's fair game.

Ultimately, the guiding principle for all Cat Angels is pleasure. Most of their rituals are rooted in convenience or desire. Among the finest Cat Angel attributes is their outlook: they are definitely from the glass-half-full camp. Nearly every facet of their lives is cause for celebration, and that is surely something to emulate. If you combine Cat Angel pleasure principles with daily Cat Angel observances - (namely the transient nature of life, the availability and quality of food, and the more tangible phenomena of Mother Nature and her glorious seasons) - then you've got almost the entire Cat Angel spiritual calendar laid out before you.

In the end, we may not agree with our Cat Angels as to who is in charge; Cat Angels typically claim this rank for themselves. But we can surely learn from our Cat Angels' other customs, their blissful states of mind as well as their reverent and irreverent ways. 🐾

Tenth Life

———◆———

What is it like to live on the cusp of eternity? Is it freeing to know for certain that peace and possibilities await? If life on earth is just too hard, do some Cats deliberately live their nine lives at a quickened pace? And is it our role as caring humans to help these Cat Angels make their final passage when they need our help the most?

Some of the Cat Angels who crossed my path had conflicting feelings about these issues. Many had not found a home on earth and were still hoping for that loving connection before their own final departure. Others were too frightened to search. They began their earthly lives unwanted and alone and worked hard to keep their distance. They survived on sheer stamina and stealth.

The two Cat Angels in the foreground of this image were among the more transitional Cat Angels that I met. These Cat Angels seemed to know that life on the other side was beckoning them. They knew that was where they truly belonged.

You can't depend
on your judgment
when your imagination is
out of focus.
- Mark Twain

Greenman

———— ❦ ————

Thor came from a family of devout nature-lovers. His home was nestled gently at the edge of a large, protected woodland, and he and his family regularly celebrated the advent of each season. When he wasn't reveling in the earth's bounty (the sun-warmed rocks, the catnip, and all those small rodents), he was aerating her turf while helping out with the compost.

In these ways, Thor was truly one with the earth. It also didn't hurt that he looked so darned good in green. He was one handsome ginger tom, and well aware that nature's complementary colors enhanced his appearance, especially in that lush time of summer.

A couple years ago, in a single moment, Thor traded in his last few lives during a particularly precarious street-crossing. He always knew that his time outside was rife with peril. Yet he was also of the firm opinion that automobiles were an aberration and that nature did not approve of them. He liked to think that Mother Earth preferred the feel of his paws to the tires of any car.

Thor is living among the trees in his mystical realm now, communing with nature and with his other Green Angel cohorts.

Trees are the
earth's endless effort
to speak to the listening heaven.

Buddha Cat

Something Zen. Something blue. Something saffron,
something true....

Bliss, like most cats, was blessed with a beginner's mind. He was often calm and
gently observant. He possessed a powerful sense of inner peace, contentedness,
and eternal connection with the universe. Most of all, Bliss was always grateful.

Bliss liked to use his forays into the mystical realm to further his spiritual
practice. He reveled in the here and now, wherever and whenever that was,
under the tutelage of his favorite spiritual leader, whoever that was at the
time. He was a "love the one you're with" kind of cat.

When food was scarce, Bliss didn't become anxious. Instead, he took his
hunger pains as an occasion for gratitude. He remained thankful for the meals
that brought him to his present moment of hunger. He knew he could calmly
look forward to the moment when he would give thanks for his next meal.
And he wasn't especially anxious for that next meal or for that future moment.

This serene outlook came in extremely handy for a cat who lived on the
streets. Bliss did not live in fear. He did not have to covet or envy. He simply
lived with awareness, and he admired and received with gratitude. Bliss knew
that the universe would provide.

The reason domestic
pets are so lovable and so
helpful to us is because they enjoy, quietly
and placidly, the present moment.

- Arthur Schopenhauer

All Fur's Night

Gunga Din's mystical world is full of frights and chill-filled frolics. Perhaps that is because his days in the earthly realm are so full of love and sunshine. But when Gunga Din decides to venture into the mystical realm, he searches out the thrilling, the frightening, and the inherently dangerous.

Gunga Din especially loves to visit FitzFeral's Way, which is so fraught with black holes that most Cat Angels consider it the Devil's Triangle of portals. This is where Gunga Din goes to find his Cat Angel forbears who have never quite found their rest and are still trapped in between.

As a rule, Cat Angels are too afraid to visit this site, but Gunga Din just can't help himself. He knows it's rude to rubberneck and risky to linger. Nevertheless, he continues to skirt that edge. He likes to think that he will someday befriend these tormented spirits and help lead them to the other side.

On the weekends, Gunga Din moonlights as a Cat Angel adventure guide for the mystical realm's most dangerous places. It's difficult and frightening work, but he enjoys it just the same. Gunga Din figures that rescuing a few lost souls can't be all that much harder. A little courage, perseverance, and a good cache of catnip might do the trick.

The supernatural
is the natural not
yet understood.
- Elbert Hubbard

Jenny's Box

Jenny has the eyes of love. She says her eyes are just like the big bad wolf's mouth: all the better to take in the wonders of the world.

Jenny's eyes never miss a thing. Not a butterfly's shadow, nor a snowflake's fall. She most certainly never misses the shimmering rays of a sunbeam, no matter how small.

When Jenny tires of her earthly home, she slips into her alternate reality to continue her discoveries anew. In the mystical realm, she finds each season brimming with surprise and splendor, and the sights there never cease to amaze her.

Jenny's main passion on the other side is to celebrate the seasons. In spring, she often joins in the dance of the Maypole with its inevitably confused choreography and shredded ribbons. In winter, she celebrates the decoration of the evergreens, a ceremony that never lasts long: the trees are just too much fun to climb, and the ornaments are too much fun to play with.

Jenny wouldn't bother to come back home if it weren't for her loving parents and adorable siblings. But when she does come home, she enjoys the occasional luxurious catnap in which the seasons continue their ever-vibrant march through her incredibly vivid dreams.

Let us love winter,
for it is the
spring of genius.
- Pietro Aretino

Cats in the Castle

Castle ruins were Phooka's favorite places to visit. He loved the sense of mystery and the feel of ancient history underfoot. He loved climbing the crumbling walls to reach higher vistas. All the better to surprise the unsuspecting and evade the unwelcome! Like all cats, he loved to gain that commanding perspective.

Grounds-keeper kitties patrolled these ruins, and Phooka loved to visit with them. Some were among the uninitiated, and some were self-actualized Cat Angels like him. And some of those Cat Angels were on their final mission to the mystical realm. These Castle Cats would gather and gossip about who came to visit every day, and their favorite visitors, the regulars. Their conversations were punctuated by occasionally successful mouse-chases.

Nearly all of the ruins had volunteers who came to feed the castle cats. And what a boon that was for Phooka: he got to eat whatever food these volunteers brought, and it showed. I always wondered where Phooka's extra pounds came from. They couldn't possibly all have come from my own earthly kitchen.

The eyes indicate
the antiquity of the soul.
- Ralph Waldo Emerson

Moon & Star

Moon and Star are forever dreaming on the darkened branches of either world. Theirs is an elaborate pageantry. As moon and star, they are constantly moving and changing, at the same pace as their celestial cohorts. They wax and they wane. They mimic the form and dance of the zodiac. They reflect and they twinkle, then quietly dim until nearly imperceptible.

When their earthly realm suffers the full onslaught of day, Moon and Star slip into the mystical realm. After all, night is a better time for prancing about with a heightened sense of mystery.

To be a star, you
must shine your own
light, follow your own path, and
don't worry about the darkness,
for that is when the stars
shine brightest.
- Unknown

Rites of Spring

Every spring, Furry gathers the usual suspects: Jenny and Gunga, Jackie and Jesse, Sweet Pea and Tippy. Together they trumpet the return of the most riotous season in dance and song. Tuxster usually sits this one out.

What Furry loves best about this celebration is how incongruous spring can seem. As they dance, Furry and her friends lovingly hold spring's most delicate flowers in their paws. But as delicate as they may appear to be, these flowers signify the incomparable strength of the earth and her triumphant return to glory.

Furry looks forward to the spring celebration each year. And when it doesn't come soon enough, she schedules it early; sometimes she'll even schedule a spring celebration several times a year. If a Cat Angel wants it, she can have spring year-round in the mystical realm.

The earth
laughs in flowers.
- Ralph Waldo Emerson

Wizard Cat

Mouse was perhaps the luckiest of cats. He was certainly among the most cuddled. His human family was so creative, sporting, and well-read that Mouse had no end of inspiration for his many jaunts into the mystical realm.

Mouse's favorite human-boy was always in on his schemes. Together they would dream up where Mouse would go and what he would do when he got there. And Mouse would always return and tell the boy about all that he saw.

In the mystical realm, Mouse was usually a wizard, but sometimes he'd diversify. Sometimes he'd try being a gondolier or a spelunker or even a batter, with all the bases loaded. In the end, Mouse always came back to being a wizard. His boy made him feel like magic so he couldn't resist the role.

Mouse is a full-time wizard now. He casts spells on unsuspecting humans through the most unlikely of portals. And he often peers in from time to time to see how his human family is doing without him.

Just so his boy wouldn't feel too sad about his final departure, Mouse sent a new kitten in his stead. Little Furrari is orange, and he's whimsical. He's patient and he's malleable. And now that he's old enough, Furrari takes little field trips into the mystical realm to learn from the best. Mouse wouldn't let just any old Cat Angel near his human boy. So he's teaching him all that he knows.

If you have built
castles in the air,
your work need not be lost;
that is where they should be.

- Henry David Thoreau

Fallen from Grace

Cat Angels leave paw-prints on our hearts. But sometimes they'll shred our favorite furniture or puke into our shoes. They might even clean their private parts in front of company or play Humpty-Dumpty with our prized possessions and then pee on the carpet for good measure. Even a spiritual guide needs to vent once in a while.

But as hard as it is to imagine, we can learn from these less-than-graceful experiences.

First, perhaps we should take nothing for granted. Maybe that isn't really our chair after all? Better work on those attachment issues.

Second, shouldn't we all know by now that nearly everything in the world is a toy as far as Cat Angels are concerned? And it doesn't matter to them whether we agree or not.

And there may be a wonderful third lesson we can take from all this. We, too, can learn to live in the moment just as our Cat Angels do: with complete abandon!

While we're at it, why not exploit every opportunity for excess? There's always room for redemption later on, just before dinner time. 🐾

Secrets

Maggie, Maggie, Maggie. Won't she ever learn? She's always taking the low road, no matter what world she's in.

Maggie is forever spreading rumors, creating storms of protest, and sowing discontent wherever she goes. And all the while, she's projecting: the very qualities that Maggie claims to detest, she has within herself in abundance. As we all know, projection is a lazy way of confronting one's own demons. Maggie is aware of her hypocrisy but she enjoys it.

Clearly, Maggie has a promising career in feline politics. Her reputation for spin is unprecedented in both Cat Angel realms. She has even been courted by the shadiest members of human government. But Maggie much prefers her own furry-feathered kind—as well as the sensation of being a big catfish in a very small but sensational pond.

Some day Maggie intends to stop her hurtful ways, but for now she just can't quit them. It doesn't help that her minions have such a voracious appetite for her most terrible tall tales. Maggie insists that supply must meet demand, and she certainly doesn't want to disappoint.

There is only one
thing in the world worse
than being talked about, and that
is not being talked about.
- Oscar Wilde

Catty Corner

In the mystical realm, Miss Kitty hangs out with the worst sort. But back home, she is perfectly good, well versed in music and literature and spoiled by the prettiest wildflower gardens, as well as the softest of laps.

When Miss Kitty ventures to the other side, all hell breaks loose. No more politeness. No more prose. No more prissy pontification. Once she's crossed over, she's all provocation. She becomes the consummate delinquent.

Miss Kitty is forever aiding and abetting the silliest of petty crimes. And she always gets away with it, too. No-one ever suspects the sweet white kitty with the pretty green eyes....

A white wall is
the fool's paper.
- French Proverb

Little Tiger's Revenge

Little Tiger's human parents were obsessed with golf. They went on golf outings every weekend. They watched golf on TV. They had golf-themed magnets on the refrigerator and goofy golfy kitsch all over the house. (And not nearly enough cat-themed things, if you asked Little Tiger.)

Little Tiger tired of hearing wasted words that should have bespoken affection for her. Instead she was subjected to the same old litany each day: eagle and birdie, big dog and dogleg. Hog, fish and frog hair. Scruffy and wolfman. Blah blah blah.

So Little Tiger took it upon herself to exact sweet and stinky revenge. She always made it a point to pooh-pooh the whole golf thing whenever she had the chance. Fore!

Golf is a
good walk spoiled.
- Mark Twain

Too Much Fun

Soozie can't help herself. In her everyday home, she's quite the loner. She tends to go solo, skirting most cat gatherings. Otherwise, she might resort to stalking and battering her cat-siblings. Poor Soozie never learned how to play well with others, and it shows.

To make up for this personality disorder, Soozie uses her jaunts into the mystical realm to let it all hang out. She drinks catnip ale until she loses her inhibitions. Once she's gone all bubbly, she dances and sings and staggers about. At that point, Soozie becomes a simultaneously endearing and nearly unbearable sweetheart at last.

Most Cat Angels consider catnip abuse annoying. But they do tend to cut Soozie a little slack when she gets to the other side. The girl clearly needs to learn how to relax and socialize. Her catnip junkets seem to be her only ticket. When Soozie does go overboard, her buddies just shuttle her back to the everyday world so that she can sleep off her catnip stupor in the safety of her own bed.

It is not abstinence
from pleasures that is
best, but mastery over them
without being worsted.

- Aristippus

Hookah Bo

Some habits die hard. And just as he is on earth, Bo remains a Nip-Head in the mystical realm.

Bo has got it good in his earthly home. He never goes without. His parents spoil him silly, and he's treated to an endless supply of catnip.

Even so, on the other side, Bo becomes ecstatic. His favorite hang-out is Hookah Bo's—of course, that's probably because he founded the joint. In that fine feline sanctuary, Bo and his buddies enjoy what is probably the most popular form of catnip delivery, the communal catnip hookah.

The road to excess
leads to the palace of wisdom.
- William Blake

Couch Potato Molly

———⊰•◦•⊱———

Some say that Molly is a sad excuse for a Cat Angel. She has just as much opportunity to explore as the next cat but she chooses to go no farther than her own cozy chair. She just won't budge, no matter how many crumbs she's dropped onto the upholstery.

Molly's Cat Angel buddies are concerned: they think she has no aspirations and is completely indolent and apathetic. They see no evidence that she has exercised her freedom to explore the other side.

"Not true!" protests Molly. For Molly has conveniently found a window into the mystical realm within the screen of her own television set. She may not exercise her freedom in the traditional sense, but she does love to live vicariously through the exploits of others. Reality can be just too uncomfortable. It's better to watch it on TV. Besides, chair cushions are soft for a reason.

It takes a lot of time
to be a genius, you have
to sit around so much doing nothing,
really doing nothing.
- Gertrude Stein

Cat-Moon-Do

These cats are taking the car and they sure as heck aren't going to the vet's! There aren't any vets in the other world, anyway. There's no need, as no one truly gets hurt over there.

But sadly, it cannot be said that no one gets offended. And these Cat Angels are well aware of that fact. They discovered early on that they can get away with anything in the mystical realm. So they do that on a daily basis.

These fallen angels are always together, always obnoxious, and always irresistible. When they tire of showing off, they go back home to their earthly homes to rest a while. (Being obnoxious can be very exhausting!) Once they have recharged, they rush back to the mystical realm to raise more ruckus. It's what they do best.

Exuberance is
better than taste.
- Gustave Flaubert

Angel Traditions

Love & Learning

—◦▸◦◦◃◦—

These are the traditions that truly warm the heart. They are so much like our own: look at how much we have in common throughout the stages of life. We all grow and we play. We care and we love. We learn and we teach. We sleep, perchance to dream. And some of us even learn to fly.

In these traditions of living, loving, and learning, we and our Cat Angels are practically mirror images of one another. And it's fun to admire our reflection, even if it tends to be a bit furry at times. As a rule, though, Cat Angels seem to look much better than we do when they do whatever it is they are doing. Perhaps we should preen more often? Or take more beauty-naps?

At the very least, we should continue to admire the Cat Angels in our lives. They are a beautiful sight to behold. More importantly, even their simplest acts can reveal valuable lessons and provide treasured glimpses into the mystical realm. Let us watch for them and be grateful. 🐾

Peace Angel

Some Cat Angels use their mystical time to pay penance for past wrongs. If they aren't merely creating the semblance of piety, they are out there doing genuine good deeds. These cats may be angels but they still have that enduring bad rap for their bird and rodent fixations.

Cats Angels are painfully aware of this reputation, so they do try to be good—at least on the mystical side. When they aren't following instinct, or falling under the influence of fallen angels, most Cat Angels go out of their way to make peace with their enemies. They try to soothe their most common prey and become peacemakers among all creatures great and small.

The
greatest strength
is gentleness.

- Iroquois Proverb

Big & Scary Lessons

Mei-Mei lived high in the mountains. She daydreamed amidst the laurel and the ladyslipper. She played hide and seek inside the clouds. But despite all the beauty, the mountains on earth could be dangerous. Mei-Mei knew the perils well: coyotes and owls, rattlers, and more.

Since too many earthly cats succumb to these dangers, Mei-Mei wanted to do her part. On the other side, she gathered the younger angels around her. She concentrated her efforts on the most easily frightened, the shyest, and the most insecure. She taught these angels about the game face and the puffed-out bluff-out. She taught them all that confidence is more than half the battle.

Of course sweet and kind is the way to go. She reminded them of that, too. But she wanted these little angels to know that there are times when a little scary is in order. She urged them to pad softly but to carry some big hair.

If you have no
confidence in self,
you are twice defeated in the
race of life.

- Cicero

Three's a Crowd

Typically, a well-cared-for Cat Angel is a neutered Cat Angel. No unwanted litters, no new strays. Most Cat Angels are quite happy with this arrangement. They prefer to live without all of those cacophonous courting rituals and those countless clamoring kittens.

Nevertheless, some Cat Angels do feel as if they are missing out. Lucky for them, parenthood is only a wink away—no more need for the empty nest syndrome! In the mystical realm, all Cat Angels can parent to their heart's content. (Even if they don't do it very well!) And all kittens can be pampered and spoiled.

We never know the
love of our parents for us
till we have become parents.

- Henry Ward Beecher

Mt. Rushmeow

Foxy and Joey are loving parents and avid teachers. Every venture they make to the other side is a family affair, and every destination they choose is for educational value.

Foxy especially loves to plan their field trips. History, technology, geology....She tries to cover as many subjects as possible with each trip. And she's always certain that everyone else will be as thrilled with her choices as she is.

Naturally, there are times when the kittens would beg to differ. At their age, they figure it's their job to cultivate the appearance of adolescent apathy, so they try very hard to feign disinterest.

But try as they might, they eventually succumb to Foxy's enthusiasm. They just can't resist the appeal of knowledge and all that both worlds can offer.

No matter
how much cats fight,
there always seem to be
plenty of kittens.
- Abraham Lincoln

Head Over Heels

Everyone knows cats are naturally acrobatic. They can achieve incredible air-time when they're inspired.

But in the mystical realm, that air-time can become positively outrageous. That's because on the other side, nearly everything is enhanced, and nearly everything is possible.

Angel wings put a whole new spin on old courtship rituals. "Head over heels" is no longer just a figure of speech. And this is a great thing for normally shy and curmudgeonly Soozie. Once she's through that portal, Soozie likes to make up for all she's been missing by courting all the kitties on the other side.

You can't sweep
other people off their feet,
if you can't be swept off your own.
- Clarence Day

 Ivy League

---

Brickle can't seem to shake his attitude problem. Not that he's ever tried. He always wants it all, and he wants it now. He also wants it here as well as over there. Because in Brickle's case, he can take it with him, and he can eat it, too.

Brickle has always liked that saying, "He who dies with the most toys wins." He figures if he doesn't have enough toys, he can always steal more from his buddies. The more the merrier—toys, that is. For some reason, Brickle doesn't have very many friends.

CAT ANGELS

What's the matter
with the world?
Why, there ain't but one thing
wrong with every one of us - and
that's selfishness.

- Will Rogers

Tiptoe

As far as her parents are concerned, Tiptoe can't carry a tune in a bucket. She screeches more than she sings. And whenever she does try to sing, everyone else is sure to leave the room.

To complicate matters, whenever Tiptoe tries to play an instrument, it's a similar disaster. She tends to scratch and break things with her clumsy claws and curious teeth.

Bless Tiptoe's heart! She thinks that music is the greatest gift to all creatures. Her fondest wish has always been to make a joyful noise.

So, when Tiptoe tiptoes to the other side, that's what she does. She plays music and sings for hours upon hours—and she does so beautifully! In the mystical realm, everyone can make heavenly music—even Tiptoe.

Music gives soul to
the universe, wings to
the mind, flight to the imagination,
and life to everything.

Plato

Honoring Our Ancestors

———◄►◄►———

In the domestic world, cats are limited to marking their territory through their usual controversial methods. But sadly, a scratch or a scent is just too ephemeral to pass down to future generations.

Cat Angels have always wanted a more permanent monument to their own kind. With that in mind, certain Cat Angels took it upon themselves to erect lasting monoliths in memory of their ancestors. These stones stand in a favorite mystical field which is renowned for its endless supply of catnip. This field is always a place of reverent celebration and is among the first places Cat Angels visit after making their first passage into the mystical realm.

These monoliths, inscribed "Here Be Cat Angels" and "Cat Angels Were Here," are touchstones, and a Cat Angel's source of direction, validation, and renewal.

Sweet is the memory
of distant friends!
Like the mellow rays of the departing
sun, it falls tenderly, yet sadly,
on the heart.

- Washington Irving

Got Fur?

―――◦►◦◄◦―――

Cody is an adorable rascal. He's quite good most of the time, too. But his little bob tail and pretty blue eyes belie his occasionally mischievous nature. And his little dexterous paws can get him into big trouble—especially in the kitchen. Cody's favorite trick is turning the kitchen faucet on and watching the water flow. He likes best to do this when his human parents aren't home. That way, once they return, he gets the biggest reaction.

To make amends for his favorite bad habit, Cody enjoys doing good on the other side. He knows he's among the luckiest of cats, so he tries to share the wealth and help those who are less fortunate. Of course, not all the other cats appreciate Cody's largesse, but most of them seem to enjoy his gifts.

What wisdom
can you find
that is greater than kindness?
- Jean-Jacques Rousseau

Cattaj Mahal

It was love at first sight for Milk and Honey. These two were inseparable from the moment they met. Their greatest—and happiest—challenge in life was increasing their professions of love for one another. But before long, all their mutual preenings were not enough. Nor were the endless gifts of mice and treats and crinkle-balls. How could they outdo themselves when they had already given their all?

After several playful romps on the other side, these two finally realized that the mystical realm provided the perfect opportunity for the perfection of love. Together (for they did everything together), Milk and Honey built the ultimate palace for all Cat Angel lovers: a complete Cattaj Mahal, with a goldfish reflecting pool, jute pylons, and wall-to-wall carpeting. Even the onion dome was fully carpeted, and Cat-Angel lovers are often seen scampering around up there, chasing after one another while playing hard to get.

At long last, these two lovers truly were in the land of milk and honey. And with their love, they built a monument to love, to share with all Cat Angel-kind.

Where there is love
there is life.
- Mahatma Gandhi

Thank You

- to the parents and foster parents of the angels in this book: Jody Marshall & Jefri Wood, Michele O'Connell & Lena Troncoso, Morgan Buckli and Gawan & Dan Fiore, Fate Christian & Melanie Seaman, Amy Maloney & David Eisner, Kim Kaplan, Grace Griffith & Patrick Holmes, Kevin & Amy and Jenna & Hayes Muiderman, Susan Wilson, Jennifer Cutting, Myron Bretholz, Izolda Trakhtenberg & Rich Potter, Miles Frieden & Alan Kelly-Hamm, Beth & Danny Malk, Dennis & Polly Strank, Jody & Danny Butler, Carolyn & Peter Smith, Gray & Melinda and Mia Burchette, Peter Collins, Jennifer Murphy of The Dog and Pony Show, the fine folks at Fairview Animal Hospital, the fine folks at Pet Harmony, and Lewis & Marie Fields, and…. well….I don't need to thank myself, but you should probably know that 6 of my own sweet angels, past & present, are in here, too, and they are St. Clair, Ellis, Olson, Ryan (aka Little Tiger, who really is much cuter than that but not all that much better behaved), Phooka (in name only) & Soozie;

- to the Cat Angels themselves for crossing my path & for making themselves known and most especially for posing, playing & hamming it up for my cameras;

- to the Swannanoa Gathering (www.swangathering.com) for all the stellar music and long-time friendships it has inspired. If it weren't for The Gathering, Al and I wouldn't have stayed at the St. Clair house, been befriended by St. Clair and been convinced she had adopted us by one of The Gathering's finest artists, our friend Sally van Meter. Also, if it weren't for The Gathering, we wouldn't have been seduced by the mountains of Western North Carolina. We not only sat and stayed a spell, we up & moved there;

- to Doug & Darcy Orr and George & Melinda Stewart for making sure we made that move;

- to Peter Collins, Susanne Marcus Collins and the Susanne Marcus Collins Foundation for making that transition a hell of a lot easier and for encouraging us to fully explore & experience the mountains with our artistic sensibilities;

- to Leah & Shane Odom, of "Miscellaneous Oddiments" for use of their inspirational, Mythical Masks which appear in several of these photomontages. Aren't they fabulous? (www.mythicalmasks.com);

- to Asheville's Jerusalem Café for the beautiful back tent room which inspired Hookah Bo's;

- to Fluke for Tiptoe's cool turquoise Ukulele;

- to The House of Musical Traditions (www.hmtrad.com) for letting me photograph that Ukulele and other instruments in their very fine folk instrument collection;

- to Amy Maloney, Mary Sue Twohy, Izolda Trakhtenberg, Lisbet Searle-White, Julia & Sarah Petteway, Geoffrey Batchelder, Susan Wilson, Ginger Godard, Maggi Zadek, and Landen Gailey & Benny Elliott of Green Mountain Lodge for being the best animal lovers and caretakers when Al and I are out roaming the musical highway; and to Robin Siegel for all her animal wisdom & humor;

- to Henry & Rachel Cross, Izolda Trakhtenberg, Dave Wade, Larry Wolken, Chuck & Irene Boyer, Sue Ellen Lawton, Ray Gauss, and Ed Kelley for computer and photography-arts cheerleading throughout the years;

- to the wonderful veterinarians, assistants & technicians at Kindness Animal Hospital (Wheaton, MD), Takoma Park Animal Clinic (Takoma Park, MD) and Fairview Animal Hospital (Fairview, NC);

- to my dear, talented friends & music fans, I couldn't do this without you;

- to all the kind editors and authors who gave me so much encouragement along the way (don't give up!), most especially Allan and Kathy Zullo, and the truly wonderful Abby Bardi, without whose editing skills I may not have made this leap;

- to Dan Schuman of Lawrence Marie, Inc., for designing this leap so it looks extra-fine;

- to my family for raising me with abundant music, art, love & animals;

- to the animal rescuers, shelters and foster parents for all their hard work & endless love;

& finally

- to all the animals in our lives who teach us so much, even when we think our hearts are closed and our minds are set. These unlikely angels free us to love again, to take risks, and to get in touch with our inner-silly. Hooray! 🐾

Laughing out loud is good medicine. And so is loving.
So keep on laughing and go love some more.

No cats were off-shored or injured in the making of this book.

No kidding.
Try checking out all those other full-color cats out there.
It's a good bet most of them were not printed in the United States.

Amy White

lives and plays in the mountains just outside of Asheville, NC, with her husband Al Petteway, four shelter cats, and the two best rescue doggies that money can't buy. For more information on Amy and Al's artistic and award-winning musical endeavors, please visit: **www.AlandAmy.com**.

Want to share this book with your friends?

You can order more copies of CAT ANGELS from:

AtlasBooks
www.atlasbooks.com
1-800-Book-Log
1-800-266-5564

For more information, visit:
www.catangels.com

CAT ANGEL
P R E S S

CAT ANGEL PRESS
P.O. Box 2267
FAIRVIEW, NC 28730